My HOLY HOUR

St. Joan of Arc

A Devotional Journal

Season: _____

Date: _____

Belongs to: _____

My Holy Hour - St. Joan of Arc is part of the *My Holy Hour Women Saints in the Church Series*. She is the patroness of France, captives, soldiers, and those ridiculed for their piety. The cover image depicts the oil painting Appearance of Sts. Catherine and Michael to Joan of Arc (1843) from *The Life of Joan of Arc* Triptych by Hermann Stilke and is located in the Hermitage Museum.

Go to our website for a free copy of
How to Use a Prayer Journal during Holy Hour
www.HolyHourBooks.com

Holy Hour Books
P.O. Box 430577
Houston, TX 77243

My Holy Hour Devotional Journals

ISBN-13: 978-1-093385083

First Printing: 2019

Holy Hour Books is an imprint of Ordinary Matters Publishing.

Printed in the United States of America

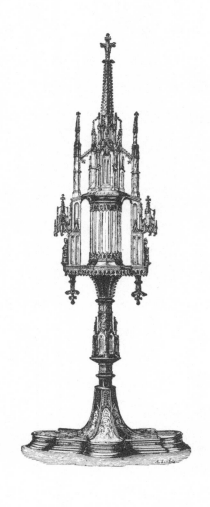

"Act, and God will act."

— *St. Joan of Arc*

Why Keep a Holy Hour

"First, the Holy Hour is not a devotion; it is a sharing in the work of redemption... our Lord asked: 'Could you not watch one hour with Me?'. In other words, he asked for an hour of reparation to combat the hour of evil; an hour of victimal union with the Cross to overcome the anti-love of sin.

Secondly, the only time Our Lord asked the Apostles for anything was the night he went into his agony... As often in the history of the Church since that time, evil was awake, but the disciples were asleep. That is why there came out of His anguished and lonely Heart the sigh: 'Could you not watch one hour with me?' Not for an hour of activity did He plead, but for an hour of companionship.

The third reason I keep up the Holy Hour is to grow more and more into his likeness. As Paul puts it: 'We are transfigured into his likeness, from splendor to splendor.' We become like that which we gaze upon. Looking into a sunset, the face takes on a golden glow. Looking at the Eucharistic Lord for an hour transforms the heart in a mysterious way as the face of Moses was transformed after his companionship with God on the mountain. Something happens to us similar to that which happened to the disciples at Emmaus. On Easter Sunday afternoon when the Lord met them, he asked why they were so gloomy. After spending some time in his presence, and hearing again the secret of spirituality - 'The Son of Man must suffer to enter into his Glory'" - their time with him ended and their "hearts were on fire." — Bishop Fulton Sheen

My Holy Hour

How to Keep a Holy Hour

"I have found that it takes some time to catch fire in prayer. This has been one of the advantages of the daily Hour. It is not so brief as to prevent the soul from collecting itself and shaking off the multitudinous distractions of the world. Sitting before the Presence is like a body exposing itself before the sun to absorb its rays. Silence in the Hour is a tete-a-tete with the Lord. In those moments, one does not so much pour out written prayers, but listening takes its place. We do not say: 'Listen, Lord, for Thy servant speaks,' but 'Speak, Lord, for Thy servant heareth.'"— Bishop Fulton Sheen

"Know also that you will probably gain more by praying fifteen minutes before the Blessed Sacrament than by all the other spiritual exercises of the day. True, Our Lord hears our prayers anywhere, for He has made the promise, 'Ask, and you shall receive,' but He has revealed to His servants that those who visit Him in the Blessed Sacrament will obtain a more abundant measure of grace." — St. Alphonsus Liguori

Holy Hour Pages

"The purpose of the Holy Hour is
to encourage deep personal
encounter with Christ."

— Bishop Fulton Sheen

My Holy Hour

My Holy Hour

My Holy Hour

My Holy Hour

My Holy Hour

My Holy Hour

HOLY HOUR QUOTES

"Saint Joan of Arc, courageous woman soldier, called by God to fight and save your country from the enemy; grant that I, like you, may hear God's cal in my life and have the courage to follow it faithfully, as priest, religious, married or single.

May your motto: 'My God must be first served,' be mine also; so that through me, He may build His kingdom here on earth.

Intercede to the Master of the Harvest, that He may send laborers into His harvest.
Saint Joan of Arc, pray for us. Amen.
—Prayer by Sisters of St. Joan of Arc

"I would rather die than do something which I know to be a sin, or to be against God's will."

—St. Joan of Arc

"Oh God, Who has so loved France, You have raised up this unique Joan of Arc. We beg you by Jesus and Mary to make us share in her clear good sense, her hardy courage, her freshness of soul, her joyous gift of self, her willingness to serve You and her lively love of Your Son and His mother. Amen."
—St. Joan of Arc Inspired Prayer

Record Your Favorite Quotes Here

REFLECTIONS

Personal Index

_____ *Pgs* _____

_____ *Pgs* _____

_____ *Pgs* _____

_____ *Pgs* _____

_____ *Pgs* _____

_____ *Pgs* _____

_____ *Pgs* _____

_____ *Pgs* _____

_____ *Pgs* _____

_____ *Pgs* _____

_____ *Pgs* _____

_____ *Pgs* _____

_____ *Pgs* _____

_____ *Pgs* _____

_____ *Pgs* _____

_____ *Pgs* _____

_____ *Pgs* _____

_____ *Pgs* _____

_____ *Pgs* _____

_____ *Pgs* _____

_____ *Pgs* _____

_____ *Pgs* _____

_____ *Pgs* _____

HOLY HOUR JOURNALS

Thank you for your interest in *Holy Hour Journals*. Discover more about using journals to deepen your prayer life by going to our website and getting a free copy of

How to Use a Prayer Journal during Holy Hour
www.HolyHourBooks.com

The Holy Hour Devotional Journal Series has been created to help Catholics from all walks of life to discover, explore, and enjoy the many rewards from a deeper connection to Christ.

Like our Facebook Page:
https://www.facebook.com/HolyHourBooks

Made in the USA
Las Vegas, NV
28 January 2024

85010024R00080